The
PIMP
Playbook

The Psychology Of Pimpology

VOLUME #2

Written By

Delano B. Gurley

"Purse First, Ass Last"

-Pimpin Ken

The information provided herein is stated to be truthful and consistent, in that any liability, in terms of inattention or otherwise, by any usage or abuse of any policies, processes, or directions contained within is the solitary and utter responsibility of the recipient reader.

Under no circumstances will any legal responsibility or blame be held against the publisher for any reparation, damages, or monetary loss due to the information herein, either directly or indirectly. Respective authors own all copyrights not held by the publisher.

The information herein is offered for informational purposes solely, and is universal as so. The presentation of the information is without contract or any type of guarantee assurance.

The trademarks that are used are without any consent, and the publication of the trademark is without permission or backing by the trademark owner. All trademarks and brands within this book are for clarifying purposes only and are then owned by the owners themselves, not affiliated with this document.

Enjoy The Wisdom Contained In This Book?

@theprofessorofpimpology

All Wisdom Works If You Work It!

The Definition Of Pimpology

Pimpology refers to the study of Pimping and the psychology behind it. Pimpology teaches principles that show you how to control and manipulate others, by understanding the principles of human psychology.

Pimpology is effective because most people have no knowledge of brain psychology. This makes their minds extremely vulnerable to those who understand the basic principles. Pimpology is the study of these basic principles.

These principles make up the techniques and mindsets learned in this wisdom. And these principles named Pimpology empower an individual to manipulate the minds of others and move them into action.

This is what Pimpology is and what Pimpology does for the individual who becomes a Master. The one who studies Pimpology will be rewarded greatly with the knowledge and self and others, therefore learning the habits of the human mind as a result of his own mind.

The Table Of Pimping

"What gives the pimp an advantage over her is that he completely flips the game on the woman's head."

-The Professor of Pimpology

The Player, The Pimp & The Mack

<u>A Player</u> - He wants **Sexual Gratification**

- He wants to sleep with as many women as possible
- He uses game to get women in bed

<u>A Mack</u> - He wants **Power**

- He wants power because it brings sex and money
- He uses all his skills to get people to submit to him

<u>A Pimp</u> - He only wants the **Money**

- Not interested as much in the pussy
- He uses his mind to guide his women

"Nice Guy", Learn From The PIMP Game

Nice guys, you are the most manipulative and dishonest type of guy that exists in the kingdom of men. You say the opposite of how you really feel or even worse for you, you say nothing and just hold it inside.

Why are you this fake character in life, in bondage to your need to please and be liked? You're a people pleaser and self sacrificer who has a hard time being disliked. Fuck that! Those days are over if you want to do any kind of pimping.

If you don't like yourself, it doesn't mean shit if anyone else in the world likes you. Odds are they won't like being around you if you're needy and need the constant attention and approval of others. In this game confidence is everything! You hear me?

Your problem is:

• You're afraid of conflict so you back down because you "Don't like to fight"

• You need others to "Like you"

• You need everyone to approve of your dreams and ideas

• You always have friends around you "You don't like to be alone"

• You let girls say whatever they feel, but you avoid speaking your mind because "You don't like to fight"

• You let women set the rules and you let her control the direction of the relationship

• You do things you don't want to instead of saying no, then complain in your head about it

• Everything you do and think about centers around getting women or having sex

You don't understand who you are as a man. So instead of saying how you feel when you feel it, you hold onto it and make an excuse for yourself to be okay with it. Stop! You let the nice guy "Character" lead your life instead of your manhood leading your life.

So you need women, your family, your friends and everyone else to validate you as a "Nice man" instead of a "Powerful man". And you know what most women do to "nice guys" right? Look at your past experiences, did she not use you and abuse you?

Did she then not find her way out the door with the next guy she was talking to, while with you on social media or dating apps? See "Nice guy" All she has to do is stroke your ego, remove your defenses and take advantage of your weakness to sex.

Just as a black widow uses seduction to weaken its prey and as Delilah seduced Samson for her gain. Ultimately only leading to the loss of freedom and life for the man who fell into the hypnotic rhythm of her seduction trap.

When you act super nice and friendly all the time, women can sense this "nice guy" vulnerability in you. She can see and feel how insecure and uncomfortable you become, when powerful and confident men are around. Women are so intuitive she can feel your energy shift.

You can have a lot of women as the "nice guy" but let me be the one to be honest with you, they're all using you for your benefits. If you're okay with trading your time, attention, money and sex for free just for pussy, you're a trick.

That's the other side of the game, so pimping ain't for you. Just keep on tricking, thank you, you keep the game alive. Nice guys attract masculine girls because opposites attract. You attract a masculine woman because you're a feminine man.

Your soft, sensitive and feminine "Nice guy" energy pushes your woman to feel more masculine around you. In any two people there is always one submitting and one leading. When both people try to lead fights are created.

As a nice guy you try to overcompensate. Your only game is to use your money, your muscles, your car but never your game alone to attract a woman. Your need to be seen and to show what you have shows your hidden insecurity and your lack of confidence in your game.

Nice guys believe in love over respect. So you think that love feelings alone will keep her with you but you're wrong because her love is much less important to her than her respect. A Pimp understands that she must respect you more than she loves you at all times.

Why: If she loves you but doesn't respect you, it's only a matter of time before she'll leave you because "love" is a fading feeling. But if she loves you but respects you more, her respect can last forever even after the love fades away as long as you stay a respectable man.

You believe in a fairytale love like a woman. Love is a superficial feeling based upon how you act, so you can't rely on love because someone's love can change at any moment. You can't build your life in any way with anyone on a feeling that can change in a second.

You're willing to play the sideline or on her backup bench with all of the other simps she collects in her phone and on her social media. You'll sit around and wait for her to choose you instead of dealing with women who choose you. That's simp behavior!

<u>The Game</u>: Women only use and manipulate the "nice guy" for emotional attention. She never intends to keep you. But to keep you around she sells you dreams just as a pimp would do his hoes. Flip the game around and move as she moves.

There are plenty of "Nice girls" out here on the sidelines waiting to pay to play with a man because they're lonely and desperate. Take pussy off the table when you talk to her and put money on the table instead and watch how her game falls apart.

As a man in a world of women you need to meet a new woman and immediately think, How can she advance my future? What skills does this woman have that benefits my future? Because this is exactly all she's thinking about when she meets you and starts her interview process.

She wants your sex eventually or she wouldn't have chose up on you out of other men in the first place.

There had to be some sexual attraction in her choice of you. Once you understand how women play the game then you're equipped to play the game with knowledge.

Then once you learn the mentality you need to play the game, you're now equipped to play the game with wisdom and skill. See women have one game, and one game they play only. Women can only play the game cat and mouse.

Her pussy is the cat and your scary ass is the frightened little mouse, running around afraid of what you really want to say and feel. Believe me, she laughs with her friends about how she controls your emotions and your happiness.

Then when the fun is over, she kills your emotions by cheating with your best friend or by sleeping with someone you both knew together. This is the fate of the "nice guy". Stop being the mouse and become the cat and make her play her role, she wants to.

What's A Pimp?

A Pimp is a masculine man internally so he is always in his masculine energy regardless of how masculine she tries to act. This forces her to be in her feminine energy if she wants to interact and communicate peacefully with him.

A feminine woman wants to feel protected by a masculine man, instead of feeling masculine and having to protect her feminine man. You have to be the reason why she wants to become feminine. This is what she wants to feel like with a man she respects.

Someone will always bow down their energy to the other. No two masculine energies can exist at the same time and she has to submit or leave with the pimp. Someone will have to be masculine or feminine energy even when two men interact.

Pimps understand game! Having game simply just means you have a strategy when dealing with women, which is the result of a combined knowledge of self and wisdom of the world. The Proper Knowledge + Life Wisdom = Game.

Pimps understand the different types of games people play. Everyone has a motivation and a strategy in the game of life but not everyone's game is the same. The key is that Pimps know the mind games people play and can quickly notice when they're being used on him or others.

For example, most men use a lot of short term strategies with women just for sex. While women use primarily long term strategies with men to get the security of a relationship for themselves. Pimps use many of the same long term strategies that women use on men.

Why: Because she can't see when her own game is being used on her until it's too late because she's emotionally hooked. Once she's in "love" with you, her judgement and decision making will always be foggy with her "love" for you. Now she'll do what you want her to do for you.

Pimps also understand that women are built to take a man's energy. Her strategy is to get what you value most for her own gain. Your energy comes in the forms of your money, your resources and your attention.

A woman has her wants and needs as her priority but so does a Pimp. Just like she wants a man's energy, the pimp wants to use her energy also, not just get in her pants. Unlike most men who prioritize the pussy above everything else.

Because a pimp plays her own game against her he sets himself apart from the short term strategy of getting pussy that most men use. So ultimately he gets access to the pussy but he also gets to access her energy, her time and her money.

He gets access to her energy and her body because a pimp makes her earn what she gets. He doesn't try to wine and dine her just to get pussy like most men. He wants her to value what he gives so he makes her work for it.

This is the opposite of how most men play the game by thinking that he can earn her respect, keep access to her pussy and long term admiration if he gives her whatever she wants. But in the end he only spoils her, so she takes everything he gives to her for granted.

A Pimp understands that a woman won't value what she's given for free or all the time, nobody does. By trying to earn her approval all of the time you ultimately put yourself in the position of submissiveness to her because you're pedestalizing her pussy over your energy like a trick.

A Pimp refuses to pedestalize sex over money and self growth. A Pimp gets it clear that sex is a mutually beneficial act for her and him, not just for his pleasure by never giving her sex only because she wants it. She has to earn sex from him.

That forces her to show him that she has more to offer than her body and it removes her feelings of entitlement due to her idea of pussy power. Now without her body as her bargaining chip, she has to use her brain and her actions to impress you.

This puts the pressure on her to show she has more to a pimp than her body or seduction. She so used to using her body, her looks and her pussy to get whatever she wants out of men. Now she has a lot less confidence because she has a man in her life that makes her feel insecure.

A Pimp makes her pedestalize him and what he has to offer instead because he's highly educated and gamed up with wisdom and specific instructions for her to grow her life. He's the leader and he leads with his mouth. Now she has to follow because she can't lead with her pussy.

Every woman says that she wants a man that pedestalizes her, but she lusts for the man that she pedestalizes and she stays with a man that she pedestalizes. She wants a man that she looks up to and feels is better and more capable than her.

She really desires to submit to a masculine and powerful man she respects more than she loves. Deep inside the feminine energy wants to submit to a man so she can feel free from her cares and worries, so she lusts for a man who will allow her to be free.

Earning a man that she pedestalizes and looks up to because she feels safe and secure with him makes her feel like a little girl who won a prize that she can be proud of. This is why a man must learn that a woman's respect is much more important than her love.

A Pimp wants to have intellectual intercourse with her mind so he can take over her body. Because a woman's body will always follow her mind, not the other way around. He looks to mold his woman's mind, and not be controlled and molded by her mind.

If she molds you:

1. She'll lose her sexual attraction to you

2. You'll lose yourself

A Pimp instills his thinking in her, not the other way around. You can't allow her to program your thinking into hers, because she'll be the one in power. So a Pimp instills his thinking into her so he has the major control of her mind instead.

A Pimp only deals with women from a position of power. He understands the manipulation tricks that she uses to take power from weak men. Most men are always putting her in the major position of power over themselves because they're focused on getting pussy more than keeping the power.

Pimp.......

Love Is An Illusion

"Being in love is like being a substance abuser in need of higher and higher doses to get high."

People exalt love like it's some kind of wonderful gift from God. Why? Because it fills you with hope and warmth? You know what else makes you feel that way? Cocaine, PCP, Methamphetamines & Alcohol. You wouldn't make any important life decisions based on how a drug makes you feel, would you? I hope not!

My point is love is just another drug, not some real thing that you can base the future of your life on. The decisions that you make for love, the choices you claim in the name of love, are as irresponsible and shortsighted as the decisions you make with any addiction.

Look at the worst periods of your life, look at your regrets, and the dreams you sacrificed just for love that never worked out. I bet if you were honest about it, you could trace these problems all back to the decisions you made under the influence of love.

The first step in being free of this manipulative and destructive influence is to admit that you have a problem. Then you have to stop submitting yourself to the temporary and always changing feelings of love, and the fantasy of fairy tales.

You've been convinced by the media, movies, entertainment and business marketing that love is some reachable goal in life that once you reach everything falls perfectly into place. Love is an illusion!

Ask yourself:

When has her love feelings ever been permanent towards you? Did she stay forever like she said that she would when she was high on love? Or did she tell you that she loved you but she's not in love with you as an excuse to leave?

There's always something someone can do to make her "love" go away. Her "love" can easily turn into hate right? How did she act after the relationship was over? Did you ever believe that she would act the way she did after the relationship was over?

Let's be honest, if you're going to live in the real world and not in some romance fantasy novel, suck it up, delete your old programming about love from the movies and movies. Start thinking and behaving with logic or you're going to get played.

Seriously, give it a chance. When it comes to dealing with women, go cold turkey on the whole idea of romantic love and watch your life blossom around you. Watch all your real life dreams and goals come to life.

It's time to man up and stop wasting your time on fantasies and fairytales that never came from your heart, but from the influence of television, music, your ex girlfriends, your imagination, cartoons and Disney movies you watched as a kid.

Ask yourself:

a. How many of these movies didn't have a love story somehow involved?

b. How many movies didn't even need a romantic element to be a good movie?

c. How many tv shows, movies and music tracks do you listen everyday to, that doesn't somehow mention love or being in love?

Love feelings are the most powerful drug in the world and marketing gurus understand this. What you were told about love was a sales strategy used to get your attention. And when it comes to a woman's love it's the least genuine thing in this world.

Why: Love feelings are brain chemicals that are flowing rapidly through your brain to make you feel like "love" is in the air. These chemicals are called the love chemicals dopamine and norepinephrine. Don't believe me? Look up "The chemicals released during love feelings."

The whole idea of romantic love is a scam played on you by the media, built to get you to spend money on days like Valentine's Day, anniversaries, marriages and mother's day. Don't buy your woman anything on valentine's day or your anniversary and see how she acts.

The chocolate companies, florists, diamond companies, lingerie companies, liquor companies, movies and all of the other big companies use love and romance in some way to sell you a product. They use "love" in everything they sell you.

The allure of romantic love is simply a battle of your will against your human biology. This is why so many people fall into the trap of "loves" immediate pleasure. Especially in the beginning stages of meeting a woman you're both getting high off of love.

Love drugs you and clouds your judgement at the expense of your emotions and often your quality of life. Stand up against the false idea of romantic love in yourself. Refuse to have your time wasted ever again as a slave to biology.

Stop being a slave to the repetitive love roller coaster of she likes you a lot, then she likes you some, then she likes you none and leaves. This repetitive process isn't love, this is the manipulative behavior of a love drug addicted woman.

Women are the most addicted users of the love drug because they watch the most "love" movies and marketing. Plus women benefit the most from the love concept, because it's all about celebrating her being special, never the man. So of course she craves "love".

They have programmed her internally since birth that the goal of her life is to find her prince charming. So she acts as a butterfly floating through life looking for beautiful flowers filled with "love feelings" to fill her up.

Once the love feelings are gone and you're empty, she flutters away to find the next "love" of her life. She leaves when you're empty, frustrated and the most vulnerable. It doesn't matter if you're a rich man or a poor man, once you're empty she's gone.

These men fall for the beauty of love addicted women just as easily as you, they just get taken for millions in their divorce. What makes you any different and so unique? You think you can occupy her mind for 20, 30 years without her cheating or stepping out on you at least once?

So my advice to you is to stop taking the "love drug" all together, so your life and pimp game can be ruled by logic and strategy, instead of emotions and feelings. Then you'll pimp hard and "love" won't manipulate your game into destruction.

Women Are In Love With "LOVE"

Women are not in love with the idea that most men think of "love" as. For men love is an action, and for women love is a feeling. This means that men and women not only love differently but see "love" in two very different and opposite ways.

A man sees love in a very tangible way as in what he does for her is a display of his love. But a woman sees love in a very intangible way as in how he makes her feel and how she feels about his love is "love" to her. So a woman's love is based upon her own perceptions about what he does for her.

Her love is internal and extremely easily influenced by her control and not his. This is why so many men truly have no idea in their relationships how their women truly feel. A man thinks by him doing acts of love for her that it's going to be enough to keep her love, but it's not.

A man can give his woman everything that she wants and be an amazing guy who listens to her problems and shows up when she needs him to, but her love for him could still change because it's not based upon him. It's based upon hormones in her brain.

Women are in love with the internal "feelings" they call love that are in reality love hormones and not the actual actions of love as a man thinks. These internal feelings in the brain are caused by at least 2 what are called "love" hormones.

These love hormones she feels are named oxytocin and dopamine. Sure you can do things to stimulate these hormones in her brain occasionally. But over time the same actions that stimulated them in the first place release less and less of these "love" hormones in her brain.

She felt this "love" high from the release of the love hormones with every new man she was in a relationship with, especially in the "honeymoon phase". This is why the honey moon phase was so easy. Every time you did something for her the release of love hormones were at its peak.

But over time her brain released less and less of these hormones especially as she got used to you and what you do for her. This is why when the relationship goes bad she says I'm not in love with you anymore. All this simply means is that you don't make her feel the "love" hormone anymore.

You don't inspire dopamine releases in her brain to give her that "feeling" anymore when she sees you after missing your presence, like it did earlier in the relationship. Ultimately the reality of the situation is that her "love" feelings for you have faded and you don't stimulate her brain anymore.

You don't excite her anymore and she craves that "love feeling" again. So she leaves you or goes out into the world to look for the man that makes her "feel love" again. And once she finds him she finds herself after some time not "feeling love" for the next guy anymore also.

So the cycle only continues after multiple failed relationships but she doesn't understand why. She doesn't understand why there's no "good men" in the world and believes that it's the men instead of her "love" chemical addiction.

She takes on the victim role and then uses the men that she left in her path as the ones to blame for her lack of relationship success. But the truth is that she doesn't understand herself or her own female human biology.

She doesn't understand that what she feels is "love" never was the actual and factual describable actions of love. She was just in love with feelings, and not people. That's why she could sleep with your best friend while you're together and say that you don't make her feel "happy" or "loved" anymore.

She is chemically and hormonally driven by the brain as men and women all are. But the difference is when it comes to "love", men and women are just wired differently. It wasn't always personal, it was just he made her feel the high and excitement of that "love" feeling again for a moment.

She can blame revenge or your lack of loving her for cheating, but in her search for a hormonal high the bigger picture and who she hurt wasn't her concern. Her concern was to please herself with a new "love" high that was too hard for her will power to resist.

This is why it's so important as a man to stay tapped into the energy and the actions of a woman. You must always pay attention not to her facial expressions when you do something for her, but be paying attention to her energy when it happens. This is your master key to her true mindset.

Because when she changes what she thinks of you and how she feels about you, her love feelings leave soon after. Because her love is chemically and hormonally based upon her perception of you and what you do for her, a woman's feelings of "love" changes immediately when her mind changes.

And her changed feelings will always change the relationship. Her love is extremely fickle and based upon her internal judgement of you. If you move wrong in a way that turns her off on you and her together, her love's gone. And there's nothing you can do to turn her love back on without her help.

Her feelings of love for you and her together will change at the drop of a dime. And any false move on your behalf, will change her feelings of love towards you altogether. And once a woman's feelings of "love" for you dissipate, she'll begin looking for the next man who makes her feel that "love" again.

This is why she can say confusing things like "I love you, but I'm not in love with you anymore." A lasting relationship can't be built upon "love" hormones alone. Because then your relationship with her is built upon an easily changeable and quickly fleeting emotion.

You have to build a strong relationship based upon facts and not feelings because feelings change, facts don't. This means that you have to talk about what she specifically needs to feel loved so that she has to hold herself accountable to that standard.

By making her define what actions equal love to her, she now loves with logic, not emotion. She can't say later in the relationship that she doesn't "feel" love for you anymore based upon floating ideas in her head. She's made the specific actions you can do.

Now she can't use her "love feelings" as an excuse to leave a good relationship with a great man. Making her tell you what actions she needs to feel loved will force her to deal with the reality of love and not the illusion of love.

This means that if she says certain actions make her feel loved and if you do them, there's no way she can use excuses like she needs to find her happy, or she's loves you but she's not in "love" with you as a reason to leave.

These are both excuses most woman use to explain that she doesn't feel those love chemicals flowing through her strongly or at all anymore when she's around you. These are all just learned and repeated excuses she's heard from other women.

And because so many women use these same excuses to leave relationships with good men, they're now socially acceptable for her to use. Now if she decides to leave the relationship with you she has to take full responsibility for not accepting your love actions and now she's the problem, not you.

If you did what she said makes her feel love, and it still wasn't enough for her, then she has to redefine what actions equate to love in her life. That means that she's just a confused woman that doesn't know what she needs from a man.

She changed how she felt about what actions equate to love and that's her problem, not yours. Or she's just a cheater, deceiver and unsettled woman who can't pair bond due to her wandering eyes and desire for another man.

The better looking she is and the more pictures that she has of herself trying to look her best on the internet, the more "love" chemical options she has available to her. This keeps her from having the ability the focus seriously on any one single long term relationship fully.

She's an attention collector who preys on the desire of a man's attention to get her high of love chemicals. She's become programmed from the social media algorithm to feel the emotional and physical highs of new likes and new attention.

So it's extremely difficult for her not to cheat or to want to feel that "feeling" again. It's like a drug user whose first high is amazing. But the issue is every single time that they do that drug after that, it will never be as euphoric as the first time that high released the dopamine in their brain.

The drug user will need more and more of the drug over time just to be satisfied with the high. The same goes for good looking women, models and social media addicts. The more highs she gets from likes, loves, dm's and male attention the more she needs.

Because so many women are flooded with "love" chemicals constantly on social media they have become hardwired to be attention addicts. They now pursue external validation more than a purpose or principle like class, sophistication or having wifely skills.

Chasing the highs of likes, fame, and male sexual attention feels better to her than chasing relationships with good men. This is why the amount of promiscuous women in this society has grown exponentially.

Now showing your attractiveness to the public for attention and internet fame has become so much more frequent in this day and age. So as a man don't confuse her intimacy, her sex or her confessions of love for you with her commitment.

She can give you her body while another man has her mind. That's because she's always loved the feelings of "love" and not you. She's in love with the high of "love". And like a drug abuser chasing the next high, she will chase the high of "love" over everything.

Because to her that high means her happiness. Now when you hear a woman say "I love you, but I'm not in love with you anymore" you'll understand what she really meant. She's saying that you don't get her high anymore and she has to find the next "love" high.

And like a crackhead is always looking for their next high, she's looking for the male dopamine dealer that gives her the best and most pure high until she needs more. Then she moves on to the next dealer in the form of a new man.

Pimp, Don't Become Her Trick

"She has to see you as a God! A God is always in control of himself."

If you're driven daily by low level desires like pussy or her attention or validation a woman will easily manipulate you. Because a real pimp teaches his women how to manipulate men and she'll know how to manipulate your desires against you.

You have to separate yourself from the men that trick on her:

-Don't watch much television
-Don't keep up with sports all the time
-Don't waste time especially around her

<u>The Game</u>: These are opportunities for her to predict your time and schedule beforehand. You can't do anything that shows your weaknesses or

vulnerabilities so you can become everything in her eyes. This is the only way that you can show up as a God to her.

If you have a want, you can be manipulated by a person who knows it. And if you have a desire for anything you can be manipulated. You can't manipulate a person who doesn't show they have weakness or bad habits.

But you can lead a person who has a vice, habit or a desire they submit to. If you don't want or need anything you're balanced. Now it's very hard for a woman to find an angle to manipulate you with. Your emotions are a woman's most reliable tools to manipulate you with.

You have to be the one who can manipulate her emotions. You're her Dr Phil! Your inner insecurities and flaws in her eyes will evaporate as you push her to focus on her own flaws, inadequacies and insecurities.

She'll see you as God because she'll need you in her life to be better.

Feelings Will Cost You

If you catch feelings, your pimping game is done! Feelings fog your vision and your decision making skills will get blinded by your emotions. You're built to run off of logic, not emotions as a man. If she can get you to think emotionally she's the pimp.

Business is not about love! You cannot bring love into your game and into business. In business you can't commit to love because you have to always stay focused on the goal. Like a fortune 500 company you have to commit to the bottom line (the goal) only.

Stay focused on the facts, not your feelings. People will try to get you in your feelings to throw you off or to manipulate your decision making. Keep your decisions fact based and only make decisions that you weigh out the costs and benefits first instead of how you feel.

Let Her Invest Her Time & Money In You

"If you are doing all of the investment, she will naturally get spoiled"

The more time and money she spends on you, the more attached she will be in the long run. That's because she's made a time, an emotional investment in you. The more time, emotions and money that a woman invests in you, the less likely she'll leave that investment quickly.

This is the opposite of how most men play the game. Normally a man does all of the investing in her then he gets attached, while she isn't. He spends all of his time and money trying to wine and dine her to show her that he's worth her time.

But inevitably all he's doing is showing her that she's the valuable one in the relationship. Because a valuable person isn't trying to convince the other person of their value. They know their value and require others to invest in them.

You're the valuable one and if you want her to see you that way then you let her invest in you first. Let her spend her money on you, let her do the most of the phone calling and let her make the most effort to find time to spend with you.

Let her invest in you, not the other way around like most men think they should do. If you let her do the majority of the investing then she'll be hesitant to take a loss on her investment in you. Let her do the work to earn her role in your life, not the other way around.

Let her make time to spend with you so that her time investment is high. A woman will value her time invested in you more than her financial investment in you. So make her put in as much time investment as possible.

She'll be hesitant to give up quickly on you because she doesn't want to invest that much time and money in you and get nothing for it. If you don't keep her investment in you high she will intentionally do just enough to get you attached to her then ease up.

This is how she gets you and so many other men attached in the beginning thinking that she's wifey. All she did was let you make all of the time, money and emotional investments into her. She just played the good girl role to keep you investing in her until you were hooked.

Then later once you both got serious in the relationship she switched up her actions and her attitude on you. This is why you let her do all of the investing in you because she will always put in a lot of effort to win your approval at first.

Because in most cases a woman will always put her best foot forward on the gas pedal when she meets you because her feelings are involved. She's in the submissive role of needing your approval so she's willing to do the bulk of the effort.

But once she's gotten comfortable and her logic kicks in then she'll ease up on the gas pedal to see if you'll give back. So selfishly when she invests in you, she's looking to get back at least the time she spent on you and financially.

This is why you make her invest her time and do 80% of the effort in everything. This sets the standard for the relationship because she sees that you're the valuable one to be invested in, not just her like she's used to with most men.

Make her earn your pleasure and your company instead of you trying to earn hers. If you do this when dealing with a woman you'll get both. A man has to use the same game a woman uses on her to win. If you use her own game against her then she won't see it coming from a mile away.

Women aren't used to men dealing with them using logic, game and strategy. Because most men are dealing with her with lust and desire. Let her invest her time and money in you and you'll always reap the rewards of it.

Remember that value doesn't market itself because it's valuable and not everyone can afford it. Make her invest in your value and she'll value you, your time and your energy because she had to work for it. If she doesn't want to do the investing in you, let her go for one who will.

Stay Hard For Her To Figure Out

You are controlled by your habits and impulses. Your habits determine the direction of your entire life. And these positive or negative habits lead you towards peace of mind or a chaotic mind equalling a stressful life.

Your habits control your behaviors. Habits are emotional impulses that push you to act outside of what you think is wrong or right. These habits and impulses will make you betray yourself and your family.

The Game: Habitual impulses can be manipulated by those who pay attention that you have them. If they control what you have a habit of, they have a tremendous amount of power, persuasion and control over you.

If she can manipulate your habits then she will manipulate your mind. That's because you're giving her the game on men, so it'll backfire on you. As a Pimp your job is to teach her how to manipulate money out of a trick through his habits and she'll try these "tricks" on you also.

Example: The woman is the worm and the trick is the fish. The worm is the weakness to the fish that the fisherman manipulates by giving the fish a taste but never the whole meal. You're teaching her how to be the worm to the trick. That's why they're called a trick.

She'll learn from your game how to control a man. Now she'll know how to use a man's desires and weaknesses against him to outsmart men and control them with his lust for her. Before she met you she could only use her body to draw in a man, you gave her the game of what to do next.

So because she knows how to run game on men you'll have to always stay on your p's & q's. You'll become just like the tricks if you have vices and habits controlling you like drugs or alcohol. Because she'll use her leverage to take advantage of you however she wants.

This could mean you could get set up by her, left or even worse killed, if you don't treat her the way she wants. If she can manipulate you enough times, eventually she'll think she's smarter than you because your habits got you slipping on your Pimpin.

It's only natural that she'll use these same strategies on you to see if you'll fall for the same tricks that you've taught her to manipulate all men with. The game will become a part of her, like it's become a part of you.

Every habit you have in your life are physical and mental hooks. Your habits are emotional hooks for people to control and manipulate you with like the trick. So you can't love money or anything else because anything that you're in love with becomes a hook that can be taken advantage of.

Rise above your habits so you can be the puppet master not the puppets. This means that you have to get so logical that all you see is the strings on the puppets. Become extremely balanced and centered in your mindset and your emotions so that you're hard to read.

Get to the point where you're almost narcissistic. Have the attitude where you enjoy no highs or no lows around her. You can't have any wants, lusts, desires, dreams, goals, nothing. Because she can control your lusts, your desires, your dreams, your goals once she knows them.

She can hook into your emotions and manipulate you with these things once she knows them. Keep all of these important factors to yourself and only tell her what duties you need her to do. Even if that means selling her a false dream when she asks.

As a pimp you can't manipulate and be manipulated at the same time. You have to cut the strings of your puppet masters in the form of your habits, lusts and desires that control your emotions. This cuts you from being controlled and from any real emotions also.

Why: You have to switch off your emotional vulnerability. Emotions are what cause a pimp to make deadly mistakes in this game everyday. Think with logic and then you can add the right emotion when you need to because you're in control of your emotions.

Never Let A Ho Ruin Friendships

This is an important rule for the younger players to learn early in the game and stick to religiously. A woman will separate you from your friends, but your friends see what you can't in this game. If she separates you from your friends, then she can manipulate you.

She will demonize your friends because she sees them as her competition to your time. She will manipulate your pimping to make her more comfortable over time, especially if there's no other pimping around to straighten you up.

She wants to get you away from your friends so she can get you alone and get you dependent on her input and her feelings. Keep your space from your ho's by having solid friends to spend time with so they can miss you.

You'll be lucky if you make and keep loyal and dedicated friends in this game long term. But long term friendships will only be possible if there's a solid common understanding when it comes to conduct with your ho's and money.

The Pimping

"A ho is going to ho regardless, a pimp is simply the man who gets her to pay him for protection and care."

-The Professor of PIMPology

Control The Balance Of Power

All decisions must be made by you to keep the balance of power. Even her idea is your idea. Because if she starts thinking that she's the one making the decisions then she'll start thinking that she's the brains of the operation. You're the pimp, so you're the brains of the operation, never her.

If you keep yourself as the powerful one over her:

a. She has to be asking you questions for direction

b. She has to be the one trying to figure you out

<u>The Game</u>: When it's her idea, make it seem like she's well trained by you to come up with that idea. Say things like "you've learned well, or our brains together come up with great ideas". Never let her feel like it's fully her idea. Reframe what she says in your words to make the idea yours.

If she's getting all her answers answered then you have no more mystery and no challenge left in her mind. If she feels like she has you figured out then she'll lose her respect and admiration for you. You need her to feel like she always has more to learn from you.

You want her to always be asking you questions about you and your life. Asking you about her life and how she can make improvements or do things better than she is now. And you want her asking questions about how she can improve for you.

This means she looks up to you and respects your opinion. Once she stops asking you questions about her life, how to improve it or how she can be better for you then she feels like she doesn't need your input or you anymore.

Who asks questions?

#1. Students

#2. Amateurs

#3. Un confident People

These are all inferior and submissive mindsets. A student is only a student when there's a teacher who is respected as having more knowledge than the student. And an amateur is only an amateur when they feel like there's a professional around. An unconfident people feel lost without guidance.

In reality it's not all that important about the questions or the answers at all. It's the fact that she thinks and believes that you have the answers to the questions she's asking. It's the fact that she has a superior respect for you and feels like you know more than her.

It's very important she looks up to you for guidance in life. If she does see you as the teacher and herself as the student then she'll respect and listen to your words of instruction. This is why you stay away from hard headed women because they don't respect a pimps expertise so they won't listen.

Never say you don't know something even if you don't know. This kills the feelings that you know what she needs to know. It's better to say that you don't care about that topic because it's unimportant and she shouldn't either because it's a waste of time.

Only Accept Submission

What is Submission: Submission is when a woman stops trying to fight your thoughts and your ideas because of her initial feelings of disagreement and takes the time to actually listen to understand you instead of fighting to be right.

When a woman listens then she's submitting her own thoughts and opinions to listen to the thoughts and opinions of others. As a pimp you can't ever waste your time with a woman who can't stop talking for enough time to listen.

When a woman respects you then she will desire to listen to you twice as much as she talks. When a woman doesn't respect you then she'll interrupt you when you talk, talk over you and listen to find things to fight about, instead of listening to understand your thoughts and opinions.

Most women, especially masculine women think submission is bad because she's never had to submit to any man. She's used to having the leverage of her pussy over a man. And most men will let her be disrespectful because they don't want to lose access to her pussy.

But a pimp is willing to leave any woman at any time because pussy has no hold on his motivations. His motivation is to get as much energy from her as possible in the form of her making him money and adding to his efforts to attain his goals. Pussy isn't a rare commodity, every woman has one.

If she starts thinking that she's more important than she is in the relationship, then a pimp will show her the door so she can leave without hesitation. This always gets a woman's attention very quickly because she's used to men being afraid that she'll leave them.

Women are used to being the ones who leave the relationships. They're not used to being left and emotionally they can't handle the rejection of it. So when a pimp shows her that he isn't afraid to lose her, it actually makes her want to stay.

Submission is the only option for her to stay. If she doesn't want to submit willingly then leave. Let her feel the pain of rejection and this forces her to make a decision. Do I stay and do what he needs me to do, or do I leave and have to start over? She'll either submit or quit, that's it!

How To Make Her Submit

To make her accept submission is to leave her alone if she doesn't listen. Anytime she shows stubbornness in the areas of your needs let her know immediately that "This relationship isn't going to work for you". You can't be afraid to ever lose a woman.

The Game: If she can see it in your eyes that you're afraid to lose her then this won't work. To be a pimp in your mindset you have to get the scared and submissive man (simp) out of your system first and foremost because she can see it in your eyes if you're afraid.

Tell her that "The way she's acting won't work for you". And that "You're done with the relationship if this is how she is going to act", then leave or tell her to leave depending on the setting. Do it quickly and at that immediate time of stubbornness because if you wait until later it won't work.

Don't act all emotional and sad with tears or crying. Be stern and strong with your words but not angry. If there's people around, call her into another room immediately calmly but with strong eye contact. In these moments you can't be afraid of what others think of you or the situation.

It's now you and the woman, nobody else exists! Her submission has to come quick, or you have to move your energy and your attention on to the next chick. You don't ever want to convince a woman to submit, that ain't acting like a pimp. Like I said before, either she submits or quits!

If she accepts submission to your boundaries and shows consistency in her submissiveness to listen to your words and be respectful at all times then she's ready. She loses you if she doesn't act right. Her penalty for disobedience is losing your attention and physical presence.

This is the same game of leverage that she uses on men, but you flipped it on her. If she chooses to submit after showing you show her you're willing to leave her for misbehaving, you'll mold your boundaries into her mind.

Your job is to train her mind to check herself so you don't have to do it anymore. But you can't do this through physical force, anger or by putting your hands on her. This doesn't make her submit willingly so it always backfires.

Yeah she might stay a while but using force doesn't gain her respect. She has to desire willing submission because she won't rebel against you out of her fear. Because she's submitting out of love and respect it works in your favor. Fear creates a rebellious minded and disloyal woman.

Her motivation for submission must be her love and respect for you and not her fear of you. Any person forced to do anything unwillingly will leave eventually once a better opportunity presents itself. She has to want to submit to your standards, not be forced to.

Her submissiveness must come from the fact that she benefits greatly from submitting to you. So you have to be a valuable man or it won't work. If you're not valuable to her life, none of this works because you won't have any leverage for her to be and stay submissive to your demands.

To gain leverage and motivate her submission, <u>reward her good behaviors</u>. But only reward her good behaviors. This means that you can't be the type of man who randomly surprises a woman with gifts and attention that she didn't earn.

Treat her submission with rewards. Reward her with the things that she loves and adores by understanding her love language. Rewards keep her motivated to submit. No woman will submit long term to a man without an incentive to. But this means "only" reward her for good behaviors.

Make A Ho Earn Your Affection

Make your woman work for your:

1. Conversation

2. Time

3. Texts

4. Affection

5. Sexual Energy

6. The smiles you put on her face

Your time, energy and attention has to come with a price. If it's free eventually you'll be used up until you're left with nothing. Nobody values long term anything that comes for free, without a fee and Un earned especially a woman.

Only reward a woman when she invests in you because women get free attention from lonely men all the time. If you give her your attention for free just like all of the other men she deals with what makes you any different? You're a pimp not a regular man!

Only give her good mornings and other sweet texts when she's following your requirements to keep your attention. If she isn't following the requirements to keep your attention, she gets no free attention from you period.

This teaches her through your actions that if she wants the extras from you she has to earn it. You're the value in the relationship and she has to earn access to that value. But this means that you can't be a low quality man also. If you're a low quality man, then this won't work.

Your attention has to be treated like it's valuable, special, rare and hard for just anyone to get access to. Because if you don't make her earn your attention, she won't value it because it's free and too easily accessible. This means she'll look at your time and attention as nearly worthless.

If she can get your attention whenever she wants to, it holds no value as a reward to her. But she will look at another man's attention as valuable who treats his time and attention that way. This is why you never give her the attention and validation she doesn't earn.

No compliments, gifts or extra ordinary treatment if she doesn't earn it because she won't value it over time. Giving a woman access to your attention all of the time whenever she wants it is how you create a spoiled and entitled woman who thinks she deserves more than she does.

If you give her all access to your attention and validation then her efforts to keep you around will fade over time. That's because anything a person doesn't have to work for, makes room for laziness and familiarity. Once she gets bored with your free attention she'll look for another man's attention.

Your attention is all you have to offer her mentally. And if you don't see your attention as valuable she won't either. Women need a man's validation to feel confident. For example if she goes out into the public and no men look at her she feels unattractive, unwanted and her self esteem suffers.

Little validation and attention given freely to a woman means that she'll work harder to gain that validation from you. And once she gets the validation and attention from you she'll value it because she had to work for it.

Don't over validate her with a bunch of compliments like other men. Because a man that over validates and compliments her is not what she desires to be in a long term relationship with. These men are located all over social media and easy to find for her.

Only deal with a woman willing to put in the work. If she doesn't want to earn your attention then shake her for someone who will. Value what you have to give a woman and always make her invest in you more than you invest in her.

Making her work is less about her and more about you retaining your value in her eyes. This means that you must place real value on what you have to offer, for her to value you and what you have to give. It always has to be at least an equal exchange of value between you and her.

It must always be an equal exchange of energy whenever you're dealing with any woman. It can never be just a one way exchange if you want to keep her respect and her admiration because she'll start feeling like she's more important than you in the interactions.

By giving a woman access to your value in the forms of your time, your validation and attention you're returning that value based upon what she gives you to earn it. Giving a woman for free what she doesn't earn is a formula for creating a spoiled and entitled woman that will take you for granted.

Not even your sex should be free because it's an equal exchange of energy between two people. When a woman deals with too many simp and submissive minded men she starts to put her pussy on a pedestal because they do. But her pussy isn't special, every woman has one!

Play "Hide The Dick"

Thinking pussy first, gives her pussy power over you. It's always purse first, ass last. So you gotta be a gentleman out here, not a male escort. This means that you have to stop trying to give dick to every woman and put your focus on how she can add to your pockets instead.

If you're stuck in dick thinking, then your actions, words and mindset will be full of "I want pussy intentions". She can feel this energy easily because every man comes with the same horny dog energy. Show her the opposite energy to make her see you as different.

You can make her want your dick in time by leading with your big head instead and using strategy and self restraint. Most men act like horny dogs and wag their dick in her face even if it's in your mind. She can always tell when your dick is out mentally because most men talk like it.

Your dick has a time and a place and not every place is the time to lead with your little head. Being pussy minded fogs your judgement and can put you in the position of a trick to be manipulated by an intelligent woman. This can lead to making big mistakes with women, some can be deadly.

Don't be so motivated to get pussy that you get blinded to the facts in your face like most men. You can't think like most men if you want to think and move like a pimp. Dick thinking ruins men everyday because they look past her flaws to get the draws.

The Game: Control your dick thinking so you can take her pussy power away. Her pussy is the only game she really has to rely on to keep a man's attention. She believes her pussy is more powerful than your dick because most men act like it.

Sex is an even exchange of energy not a one sided event. She's been taught her pussy has more power than your dick, show her the facts. When you show her that you value your penis more than you value her pussy, she'll have to reconsider how much she wants her pussy over your dick.

Think of it using your common sense. She has a pussy already so it doesn't benefit her unless it meets your dick, understand that. Switch the game up on her and place more value on your dick than her pussy. Now she'll pursue your dick because she has no more power or pussy leverage over you.

Remember you're switching the game up on her and using her own manipulative sex game on her. She uses sex and the fantasy of getting sex from her to get money, clothes, time and energy from a man all the time. She doesn't know what to do when she meets a man who treats her like a trick.

Every man in her past has given her sex when she wants it. So she's used to being in control of when and where she gets sex, but now you're in control. Don't give her sex whenever she wants it. Make her wait and show you why she deserves to get dick from you and now you're the ho and she's the trick.

Put Your Dick Away Until You Get Paid

Put your dick head away and pull your thinking head out. Then put your hand out for your payment. This is how a superstar in the Pimp Game moves. That's because a pimp understands the dynamics of a woman and the average man.

A pimp understands that when a woman gives you pussy she sees giving you pussy as payment. So if you give her dick she'll feel like she's even with you and she'll also feel more powerful than you because you give her your energy during sex. You give her your seed that gives life and your stamina.

Because a man can't just take pussy from a woman without going to jail, inevitably she "gave" you some pussy. In the process of sex she gave you pussy which is free to her for your real value in the form of your energy. And most men give her their money and access to a relationship for pussy.

So she sees them as a ho sees a trick. A trick trades his money and his time for her pussy so why would she see you as different? A ho doesn't respect a trick in any way. That's why it's so important for a pimp to learn how to play "Hide The Dick".

If she isn't doing what you want her to do and adding to your life in some way other than sexually, don't give her dick when she wants it, avoid it. You have to use your dick as a bargaining tool as women do all the time to men.

The Game: Use her lust against her by reversing the game and making her want your dick. If you know how to please her sexually and make her orgasm then your dick is more important than her pussy in her eyes. But if you can't satisfy her sexually then your dick has no leverage.

The little head will make a fool out of the big head if you lead with it. Because a woman knows very well how to manipulate and persuade your little head. All she has to do is touch it and make it hard to get you thinking with it. Women don't work the same way. Her mind has to be stimulated first.

Leading with the little head is what makes all of the mistakes in a man's life. So the big head has to always save the little head from trouble. The only way to prevent this is to focus on getting money, her energy in the form of her submission and her work on your behalf over her pussy.

Give her guidance and instruction instead of sex then let her pay you for your knowledge, not with her body but with her pockets. Let her share her money with you because she's looking for someone to share it with anyway.

She's looking for someone to encourage her and she'll pay for it. Show her with your words and actions that pussy isn't your primary motivation, money is. A pimp is simply a motivator, a life coach and a guide for the women who want access to his energy.

Plus she doesn't know how to master her mind and her money without the guidance of a man because she's an emotional spender, so it's better in your hands. Give her game for her money because the game doesn't come for free, only for a fee. If you give her knowledge, she'll give you her money.

<u>The Game</u>: Make it clear to her that you need payment in the form of money in exchange for her feelings of appreciation, not pussy. Mention sex is good but you're focused on building your business, your life, etc and you have to put that over everything right now. That's mind pimping!

Not even your time is free. Make her wait for your time if she can't pay for it. This way she'll feel privileged when she gets some of your valuable time because she had to earn it. Be unavailable sometimes and mention that you help other people who pay, your valuable time has to be paid for.

She will try to give you pussy instead of money to test your strength. She may even try to talk about sex to get you aroused so you'll change your mind. This is all her game! If you pass this test and make your time hard to get unless she pays for it, she'll give you money for your time.

You get to decide to get the pussy later if you want, but that'll start making her challenge you on payment terms. Don't forget that she thinks that her pussy is payment because for most men it is. So if you get pussy you could ruin the whole game, especially if you get into a relationship with her!

Don't Act Excited About Getting Paid

A Pimp has got to always be cool and maintain his calm composure when dealing with women. Especially when she's handing over her pay. The earlier that you realize that she's supposed to pay you, the sooner she'll see that her destiny is to give you her money.

Don't get excited or act grateful for her paying you. You're the pimp and this is what she's supposed to do as payment for your game. If she wants what your pimping offers, she has to pay what she weighs, if not she can't stay or interact with you another day.

It's her privilege to pay you for the wisdom and guidance that your game provides for her, versus before she met you. Where would she be without your game around to save her from her and her own mind? Definitely not where she's at now and not living as good as she lives underneath your wisdom.

A woman wants to feel like she has guidance and leadership in her life because the burden of the world often wears a woman down. So when she pays you it's what she's supposed to do because what you have to offer her is more valuable than money.

Lead Her With Words & Honey, Not Money

She will expect you to keep up the ways you try to impress her. So from the beginning set up a standard you can live with. Never set up an unreal standard because it always comes back to hurt you when you can't keep it up.

This means that whatever you lead with, is what a woman is going to respect and expect because a woman is always measuring your worth in her life. So if you show your worth is money by trying to wine and dine her with expensive dinners and gifts, she'll see you as a trick.

A trick always leads with his wallet because he's willing to give up his value just to have sex with her. So inevitably the trick loses because he gets played for his money and his gifts until it's over. In reality she only fell in love with his money and gifts, not him, his game or his personality.

She never learned to respect him as a man because she was blinded by the money and gifts. So the gifts and the money is what she respected because that's what he showed her was his value and his contribution to her life.

A woman never respects the man who tricks off his hard earned money for her, just like a ho never respects the trick. This means if you lead a woman with your wallet then she'll never respect you, or your words because she'll respect your wallet.

Even when you talk she won't really desire to listen unless money or gifts come along with your words in some way because there's no incentive for her to listen to you. So she's not submitting to you, she's submitting to the money and that's it! Once the money and gifts are gone why would she stay?

By leading with your wallet and spending your money in exchange for time with her you'll never get your money's worth for it. You'll only end up being used and feeling resentful because she never developed respect for you. But it's not her fault because you tried to win her approval with money.

Your words must always lead the way and not your wallet if you want her to respect you for who you are. You're not a trick who pays what he weighs. You're a pimp and you can never pay anyone to stay. Your game is what leads the way and because you're the value in the equation she pays you to play.

A woman who listens to your words and believes in you is the worthy woman to keep around. That's because your words are more likely to last a lifetime than your money. Money comes and goes, but it's the game that comes for free out of your mouth that she must desire to follow.

Never Negotiate With A Ho, Let Her Go

When she says she has a better offer from another man, or an opportunity to leave, never get mad, open the door for her to go. Because in most cases what she's really saying is she wants you to give her a reason to stay with you.

This already lets you know that she's looking outside your pimping at other men. This means that her eyes are already wandering towards other men and one of her feet are already out the door. She will leave eventually, if not now later.

Don't lash out or get angry even if it's your first instinct. Even if she just talks about leaving you in the first place she's already halfway out the door, so let her go and prevent yourself from the future problems of her leaving you unexpectedly.

Women are extremely picky and fickle. That's because women are built to function on 99.9% emotions and so she'll leave for the dumbest reasons, or she'll leave for no real solid reason at all other than her "feelings" sometimes.

This is why a woman will say simple minded things she's leaving because she's trying to find her "happiness". This is a feeling and smart people don't leave a relationship based upon a feeling. A smart person leaves a relationship based upon facts and logical reasons why.

So don't get your pimping caught up on the reason why a ho left because most of them will eventually leave even if you're pimping is good. You should see yourself as a temp agency of women staff. If she leaves or talks about leaving then let her leave, in fact tell her to leave if she threatens leaving you.

The better you get at this game of understanding that you can't and don't want to ever put yourself through the frustration of convincing a woman to leave or trying to figure out why she's leaving the more picky and fickle you can be about the women you choose to have access to your game.

If you have other women in your life under your pimping don't get caught up on one woman leaving. Make sure that you keep your other women in line and get back to business moving as usual.

<u>The Game</u>: If you feel the need to get her back in some way, have a leaving party without her and about her with your other women. Have a lot of fun and celebrate big time when that ho leaves. Then have one of the women go back and tell her about the party so she feels shamed.

Then if another woman is thinking about leaving in the future, she'll know you and the other women will laugh at her leaving. Then celebrate and have a major party about her leaving your pimping. One ho to go, won't stop no show. The show always goes on!

No Favoritism In This Game

The one problem a pimp will have when you have a dedicated ho that's down ten toes and stays for a long time is that you start to like her. And sometimes you'll even love and care for her more than the other ho's. So when this ho's get out of pocket, a pimp tends to take it personal because you have history together.

Remember this above all, it doesn't matter how long you've had the ho and she never got out of pocket. It doesn't matter how much game that you and the ho kicked together. When she eventually does get out of pocket, if you show her weakness the other ho's will see this and take advantage of her, as your weakness.

The Game: So always be consistent in your punishment with all of your ho's evenly or you'll start losing their respect, their body and your bread. The women are always watching you very closely to see if you treat one of the other ho's better than the other.

If they see you treating one better than the other then they will mutiny on her because they know that you're soft on her and hard on them. This only creates resentful ho's who will start entertaining thoughts of rebellion on you. Now they're vulnerable to other men and other pimps.

Know Her Mind

"Get a ho thinking in newer ways, that lead her into brighter days."

-Pimpin Ken

With No Instruction, She'll Find Self Destruction

We all need direction in our lives, especially a woman. This is why she craves the leadership of a strong man in her life. Any woman without instructions or guidance in her life will end up anywhere which is ultimately nowhere.

She has to be given direction and instruction from someone, why not you? Because any woman without instruction in her life is headed for a crash course in self destruction. When she has no male leadership she's easily led by the beliefs all the rest of the lost and chaotic minded women have.

Her natural gravitational pull is towards group thinking. That's because women are followers of the tribe by nature. She wants to fit in and be accepted by other women. So if she's not led by the thought of impressing her man, then she'll be led to impress the group of most self destructive women.

The Game: It's your job to help her avoid confused thinking and recognize the chaotic group thinking that most women easily fall into. Make your directions and your visions clear and specific with her. This will prevent her from getting lost in the pressure to be like other women.

Have her develop a mission and a vision for her life. Add to it and guide her into strategically making your vision her vision. She needs to feel like it's her vision even though it's your vision because she'll have a hard time thinking of one herself.

Just like any successful Fortune 500 company or business has a mission and vision statement, have yours and hers as one. This creates a team thinking bond and cohesive mentality. Any disobeying behavior of the vision will make her feel guilty.

Even if she thinks of doing wrong she'll think about the goal and the vision in her mind. Especially if the instructions are hard wired by time, having the mission where she can see it everyday and reinforcing her obedience to the vision with rewards for her dedication.

It's very important that you reward her obedience to your instruction. This creates a mental, physical and emotional obedience to the vision you've established for her. Using things she wants as a reward and incentive for her loyalty makes her feel accomplished and helps her stay motivated.

You can't expect any woman to stay obedient to the vision without clear instructions and the incentive in the form of rewards to stay motivated. Because if you don't give people you're in charge of instructions they'll run on their own program.

Good leaders always give good instructions. This is the measure of their leadership. And good leaders also always follow the instructions that they give because they're the first believers in their instruction. You must live as you demand her to live. That's why you have to give her "your" vision.

So practice what you preach and follow your own instructions or she will not. If she sees that you don't follow your own instructions she won't either. And you'll lose her respect for your instructions, your game and your pimping.

She needs clear and specific instructions for her to follow because they create order in her mind. And because the mind of most women are operating in chaos without order and instruction they always inevitably find self destruction.

Her disorder shows in her feeling overwhelmed, tired and exhausted by life which is what you'll find that most women without male instruction in their lives complain about. Her complaints show you that her life is in disorder and lacks instruction, so she needs yours.

Where there's disorder, there's an opportunity. This disorder in her life and her complaints about being tired and overwhelmed shows you as a pimp that there's an opportunity for you to manipulate by simply installing order and structure.

You can install this order in the form of your instructions to guide her out of self destruction. You do this by taking advantage of the opportunity to give her the guidance, motivation and inspiration that she clearly lacks in her life.

Why She Becomes A Ho

Don't believe the Hollywood narrative about why women become prostitutes, hookers, sex workers and porn stars. Of course there are women in this game who are lost and broken, but most of the women choose the game for other reasons.

The media is only try to convince you that pimping is bad or wrong based upon a few bad apples. In reality it's everyday women who want the life that a pimp who is a leader can provide. Many women get in the game just because they want a stand up man with a plan.

Dealing with the average man often leads to her being traumatized by cheaters, abusers and female users who are only interested in getting pussy. They don't bring a woman the stability, protection and wisdom that a man with pride can provide.

These things are what a pimp brings to a woman because he understands that her basic needs are to be provided for and to be protected in the world. It's not just about the money for most women in the game, it's about a man meeting her basic needs.

That's because a woman can get her own money but she needs a strong man who can make her feel safe and secure. It's also about the lifestyle and the attention that being a ho brings, not the money. If it was all about the money then why would she give it all to her pimp?

The Pimp gets all their money so it can't be her primary motivation. Some women just love the lifestyle that comes along with being with a strong man with a plan. Giving up the pussy for his benefit is just part of getting what she wants.

She's seen other ho's in her life or around her neighborhood with the money, the nice clothes and the money that made the life and the lifestyle look glamorous to her. This made her want to become just like these women.

It then becomes a psychological fantasy in her mind to be a ho because as a child or a teenager she watched classy ho's make the life look good and she dreamed of becoming just like them. She dreamed of having a pimp who upgraded her life.

And some women just really like sex, power and money. And she loves the sense of power she feels over a man who wants her sexually. She loves how it feels to be desired by a man who will do anything just to touch her. This is what drives a woman to ho and strip.

Her ability to seduce a man with how she moves her body can be like a drug for a woman. Because a woman is addicted to external validation from men. This is the theory social media is built of off. A woman loves to be flaunted, especially around other women so that they can be jealous of her.

And a pimp will make her feel like she's worthy of being celebrated, so he will dress her in fancy jewels and clothes to the envy of other women. Her desire to be in this game is either financial or emotional and sometimes both. It's not mostly women who've been molested or abused sexually.

Often it's women who crave to have a strong father figure in her life that she can look up to. Why else do you think she calls a pimp "daddy"? He is her protector and her provider just like a real man or father is supposed to provide for his little girl and eventual woman.

Of course there are women who do fall into this life because of abuse or sexual trauma. But the result for most of these women are excessive drug and alcohol abuse. An addict of a woman will never make a good ho and she will never last long in this game.

Because she will always pick her habits over her pimp just like any woman or man who has habits that control their lives. Sexual abuse and physical abuse for many women is just the common excuse women use to gain sympathy for becoming a ho.

She uses this easy out so that people will see her as a victim instead of judging her for becoming a ho in the first place. This excuse is no different from when a woman ends a relationship and it's always the man's fault.

Often it's not only his fault because it takes two people to ruin a relationship, but it's a justifiable excuse for her to not be judged for her faults. But in reality it's not a real reason to fall into the game for most women. It's just the perfect excuse to create empathy.

Sometimes she just needs startup capital for her goals and desires. Some women come into the game for only a couple of years to collect enough money to start businesses, go to college, buy a home, etc and then leave the game. There's many reasons why a woman becomes a ho, not just one!

Women Who Call You Daddy Vs Baby

Pay attention to how a woman uses her words when she speaks to you. Because what she calls you tells you how she sees you in her mind. And what she calls you determines how she sees you in terms of her desire to be submissive or dominant to you.

There's:

1. The woman that calls you daddy

2. The woman that calls you baby

The woman that calls you "baby" feels like she's teaching you. She has herself on the pedestal over you and she feels like she has more power than you. So she's faking her submissiveness to you as a form of manipulation. It's likely that she's acting feminine, but really she's masculine internally.

<u>Trust Level</u>: She's a thinker so she'll question what you say every time at least internally. So pay close attention to her actions because disloyalty is nearer than you think, she thinks too much! Her overthinking forces her to make too many moves in this game instead of the right moves.

The woman that calls you "daddy" feels like you're teaching her. She has you on a pedestal and she sees you with the power over her. This shows that she isn't acting submissive to you as a from of manipulation, she's actually submissive to you in her way of seeing you as more dominant than her.

She trusts you enough not to overthink about anything you say. She's the student and you're the teacher with the expertise that she needs in her life. This puts her at your will because she has submitted her life to your decision making. She trusts your decision making skills over hers.

<u>Trust Level</u>: You can trust her more because she needs you in her mind, so she trusts your thinking over hers. She won't overthink your words because she respects what you say. She'll do what you say because she sees it as a benefit to listen, instead of the other woman who overthinks opportunities.

The Bottom Bitch

She's The General Manager of the stable. While the Pimp is running the business, the bottom bitch runs the staff. The bottom bitch often starts out as the main ho who has absorbed the pimps game fully enough to accept it and explain it to the other women.

She's the main woman who can be trusted to keep the other women in line and to discipline the other women when they stray from the rules of the game. This is the main woman that you know is down with your game ten toes.

She's like the Queen of the women that handles the others as your stable of ho's grow. When your stable grows you might have to promote more than one bottom bitch. You'll sometimes need more than one bottom.

The more women you maintain, it gets harder to be there to keep them all in line at the same time. This means that you'll have to relay the information to your bottom bitches and she'll relay it to the other girls. This could mean that she might have her own stable of women to lead.

That means that the other girls may be her girls that she's maintaining, but they'll all pay you through the bottom bitch. This is like setting up a business franchise of working women or like running a temp service.

Each woman will have their own stable of women tied to you and paying you a percentage of profits as the owner of the stable. In reality women make the best pimps when it comes to women because she can say things in a way that a Pimp can't.

She can use the words that women use, so they'll listen to understand her. Not listening to fight like most women listen to a man. Another reason is dad wasn't always around so most women have learned to live without him. But there's always the need for a mama in her, even as an older woman.

As a man, she's trained to look at you as a trick and as the enemy to manipulate. So by having a bottom bitch doing the work for you, it can make it easier for a pimp to expand his empire. A man and a woman working together make the ultimate pimp.

Why She Wants A Pimp

Having a Pimp makes her feel safe and secure because to her it feels like his presence closes that big hole inside of her that craves the energy of a masculine man in her life that she can depend on for her base needs.

A Pimp is fulfilling an unmet past and present need. This is what a good pimp does for her. Every woman has a part of her that's missing, either emotionally or physically. She can't fill this need by herself because women crave the leadership and the energy of a man.

Give her what her parents didn't give her and that's your undivided attention. It won't matter how much money she came from, because emotionally you're giving her something money can't buy her which is acceptance and love.

A pimp in her life provides a superficially created feeling of unconditional love and unwavering acceptance that most women lack in life. That's because so many women have parents who don't pay attention to her emotional needs, only her physical needs.

The Pimp makes her feel better about being a ho because he accepts her unconditionally while the world looks down on her and how she lives her life. The Pimp gains her trust by selling her a fantasy of herself and her future security with him as something to be proud of eventually.

"Nobody will love her like you do"
"Nobody talks and listens to you like I do"
"Because nobody loves her like I do
"Nobody protects her like I do"

In reality you both need each other. The pimp needs a ho just like a ho needs a pimp. People always like to make the pimp the villain, but a pimp can't exist if he doesn't have women who are willing to ho for a variety of reasons.

Don't Act Like A Trick

A woman doesn't want to be your whole world. Because most women can't handle the pressure of being put on a high pedestal, she knows that she'll inevitably fall from. By nature women are insecure and have a low self esteem.

If you set too high of a standard for her self esteem you'll create the pressure for her to be perfect that she understands she can't live up to. So she'll eventually rebel against the need to be perfect to a lesser man who she can pedestalize.

She wants "you" to have the pressure of being perfect, not her. If she has to be perfect all the time, she can't be freaky sexually like she wants to be out of her fear of looking lesser in your eyes. She can't handle always acting like a good girl because she isn't, regardless of what she looks like.

Internally she knows she's putting up a front of being a "good girl", but mentally she thinks the same nasty thoughts as men and she'll express them with the man who lets her be imperfect and feel free to be freaky sexually.

The only pedestal she wants to be on, is the pedestal over the other women in your life. She wants to be the number #1 woman in your life to increase her feeling of security. Because her ego and self esteem is tied into her feeling like she's irreplaceable in your life.

She wants to be put on the pedestal as the star around other men but she wants you to be the star around other women. She wants other women to envy that she has you and she wants to feel like other men want and desire her. This social pedestal is the only pedestal you can put her on.

The higher you are on the social scale the more important she feels having you next to her. A woman wants a man who is like a shiny trophy that she can show off to other women and be proud of having. By nature a woman wants a man she can respect and look up to.

Never Let Her Tears Melt Your Pimping

Women are the best actresses in the world and they can turn their tears on and off very quickly based upon the reason. Crying is her go to method for escaping any problem ever since she was a child because it often worked.

If she can manipulate you easily with her tears, then eventually she'll leave you for another pimp who isn't so easily played. You must be able see through her tears by using your logic so you can hold her accountable for her manipulation.

But if you can't see through her tears and female manipulation, you're going to get pimped by your ho anytime she wants to get her way with you. If all she has to do is start crying and you'll give in, you'll show yourself emotionally vulnerable to her.

Emotional vulnerability is the worst thing to show and have in this game. There's so many negative things that a pimp sees in his life and if he's to soft hearted he'll drink or drug himself to death because of the emotional trauma.

Sometimes with your ho's you'll have to be cold as ice and use your mind instead of your emotions to see what's really going on. Sometimes you'll have to force a ho to be logical, so she can't manipulate you to get her way.

So when she starts crying, make her leave until she can talk with her brain and not with her feelings. Don't allow her to even talk to you until she can talk to you without emotions. This forces her to use her words and not her emotions.

You are the leader as their pimp. And by showing yourself as weak emotionally you'll instead get pimped by your ho's, especially if you have more than one. If she finds that you're emotionally weak, she will try you every time she wants her way.

Learn Her Desires To Know Her Devils

Women desire what she lacks in life, and she will do anything to fulfill that desire. This is why you have to gain awareness of her temptations, so you know when she'll be tempted by her desires being around. If you know her desires then you'll know when her temptations are around.

Now you can be aware of her energy in the presence of her desires. She will always go after what she desires eventually even if it's another man or another pimp. Understand that if you lack what she desires you'll lose her to it.

Understand 3 Things About Her:

#1. Her primary motivation in life?

a. Is it material things?
b. Is it emotional things?

#2. What pushes her most?

a. The pursuit of Pleasure?

b. The avoidance of Pain?

#3. Which emotion drives her everyday habits? (Faith or Fear)

a. Faith filled people are motivated by the pursuit of pleasure

b. Fearful people are motivated by their avoidance pain

Why Is This Important?

Her desires are what lead her life choices, behaviors and attitudes in life. Women who desire material things excessively or have a history of broken relationships are looking for emotional pleasure only because she desires new pleasure all the time.

She gets emotional pleasure from new things and new love interests. Anything that gets old and boring doesn't give her the rush of pleasure that she seeks anymore. And she will fill those desires even if it means hurting you.

Because her desires will constantly pull and tug on her emotions and her imagination until that desire is fulfilled. If she has a strong desire for negative obsessions like sex, money or drugs you will lose her to those desires. Negative desires have the strongest pull on a woman's mind and body.

This is why a man who gives a woman everything but what she desires will lose her to a man who fulfills that desire. For example, she could have a good man at home but if the sex is boring her desire for better sex will pull her to a man she thinks will fill her desire for better sex.

Understanding her motivations and desires helps you stay ahead of her. You'll know her motivations and you can be aware when those desires are triggered or around to tempt her. And you'll also know how to trigger those desires for your own advantage.

The Game: Use her desires for your advantage by motivating her with her desires. Use those desires as motivation for her great work, and as rewards for proper behaviors. Lead her with her desires just like you motivate a child with toys. Use her desires as motivation for her to act like you want.

The Pimp Pyramid

The Pimp Pyramid - How To Keep Her Dependent

*Based Upon Maslow's Hierarchy of Needs

The Pimp Pyramid

A Theory Of Human Motivation

• Meet her needs at different levels of the pyramid and she will dedicate herself to you

• Pimp From Level 2 the need for Safety and upwards from there

• Meet the 2nd and 3rd level while trying to find your way in her mind at the 5th level

• This is how she will devote herself to you

<u>Physiological Needs</u>
This is the most pressing of needs, which is our basic needs. We all need these things to survive and to be alive at all. This is the level of food, clothing and all the other basic necessities we need. If these basic needs aren't met, we can't even think beyond this level.

A pimp starts at this level and works upwards from there. The pimp manipulates this level once he has the down ho already, not first. He gets her dependent on him for all her daily living needs, but only once she's down.

Your Physiological Needs:

-Food
-Clothing
-Shelter

Actions:
Keep all her money for the fake "greater goal" of Level 5 (Self Actualization)

Why: By keeping possession of the money she makes, you control her basic needs

She has to always come to daddy to get what she needs. This gives her a feeling of being protected and provided for in a way a father does. That's because fatherless women crave the submission fathers demand of her.

Safety Needs

This is the area that pushes her to run towards pimps. If she was abused or mistreated by her family, she has nowhere to go but on her own or into the streets. A pimp is the perfect protection because he usually has a masculine attitude but a feminine touch with her mind.

Because he's a great communicator unlike most men, he can talk his way into her trusting him. This gives her the feelings of a father and mother because he listens to her feelings unlike her parents. This makes her feel safe and comforted by his word play and easy to talk to ear.

Use Words Like:
"I just want to protect you"

"I won't let nobody hurt you"

"I'll hurt who hurts you"

Actions:

Having guns around are an easy way to make her feel safe and secure that you can protect her body. When anyone threatens her, be the first one to stand up and say something to protect her.

The Game: Take her to places she's never been that you're very comfortable and she isn't, so she can rely on you and start trusting you

Belonging and Love Needs

This is the area most women don't get their needs met and the place where a pimp can step in easily and effortlessly. If her parents are her enemy and she has no social group, she's perfect for a pimp to catch.

Actions:

Get her to fall in love with you, by seeming as if you are in love with her. This is called creating an "illusion love".

The Game: Listen to her needs and fulfill them so she'll bond to you until dependency. Your goal is to be her only source of friendship, safety, security and companionship. The goal is also to bring her into your world of pleasure and out of her world of pain and fear.

Sometimes sexual abuse made her run so she's looking for a safe place to feel secure. Because so many young girls are molested from family members she could be running from home. Her need for safety and a place to belong makes her vulnerable to a pimp's protection.

The Game: If she's a hoe make it seem like that doesn't bother you. The average guy doesn't see a hoe as a wife candidate but you have to make it seem like you accept her unconditionally so she trusts you. You trust her imperfect self even if the world doesn't.

Use Words Like:
"I accept you for who you are"
"They don't know the real you like I do"
"I accept you"
"You belong to me"

Actions:
Look past her being a hoe, or at least act like it because if you can find a way to have feelings for her, she will reward you financially.

Ego & Self Esteem
This level determines her self esteem and value. Everybody wants to feel good about themselves, but not many women really do. All women need to feel respected, but most aren't by other women and men. This area of the pyramid will determine their level of receptivity.

A low self esteem makes her vulnerable to outside beliefs and influences. The reason pimps pick low self esteem women is because their beliefs are moldable. Some of these women with low self esteem have been touched, raped or molested. This is why some of the women in the game are addicted to drugs.

Action:
Upgrade her self esteem by listening for her weaknesses and helping her become a better her. Self esteem is hard for a hoe to find because of what she does. But don't overindulge her in validation, but give her just enough validation when she earns it that it doesn't get old.

Use Words Like:
"I'm here for you
"You're so much better than them"
"You're too hard on yourself"
"You have a bright future ahead of you"

Self Actualization

The need to feel like you can be all that you can be and accomplish something beneficial and important in your life. The feeling that you've contributed in a positive way to life and others lives.

Use Words Like:

"Right now is only temporary"

"It's just until the dream comes true"

"When it does it'll be only you and me"

Actions:

Provide a dream for the future as her way out. Keep her future right in front of her to keep her motivated, especially when she gets discouraged with what she's doing. Install in her mind a repetitive positive motto that creates positive feelings she can repeat when she's not around you.

THANK YOU FOR READING

If You Received Useful Tools In This Information, Please Give Me A <u>4-5 Star Rating!</u>

This serves as a reward for an author. It takes hours and months, sometimes years of no pay to put together books for the purpose of sharing information you see as important to the world. Please just take out a minute of your time and please leave a quick positive review.

NOTES

Printed in Great Britain
by Amazon